Taming and Training Lovebirds
KW-038

Contents

Photographers and artists: Dr. Herbert R. Axelrod, S. Bischoff, W. de Grahl, Michael Gilroy, P. Kwast, Harry V. Lacey, R. and V. Moat, Pakastina, Eric Peake, H. Reinhard, San Diego Zoo, Vince Serbin, A. van den Nieuwenhuizen, Louise van der Meid, Vogelpark Walsrode, R.A. Vowles, Dr. Matthew M. Vriends.

Front endpapers: Peach-faced lovebird. **Title page:** Headstudy of a lovely peach-faced lovebird. **Back endpapers:** Green pied peach-faced lovebirds.

1995 Edition

Distributed in the UNITED STATES to the Pet Trade by T.F.H. Publications, Inc., One T.F.H. Plaza, Neptune City, NJ 07753; distributed in the UNITED STATES to the Bookstore and Library Trade by National Book Network, Inc. 4720 Boston Way, Lanham MD 20706; in CANADA to the Pet Trade by H & L Pet Supplies Inc., 27 Kingston Crescent, Kitchener, Ontario N2B 2T6; Rolf C. Hagen Ltd., 3225 Sartelon Street, Montreal 382 Quebec; in CANADA to the Book Trade by Vanwell Publishing Ltd., 1 Northrup Crescent, St. Catharines, Ontario L2M 6P5 ; in ENGLAND by T.F.H. Publications, PO Box 15, Waterlooville PO7 6BQ; in AUSTRALIA AND THE SOUTH PACIFIC by T.F.H. (Australia), Pty. Ltd., Box 149, Brookvale 2100 N.S.W., Australia; in NEW ZEALAND by Brooklands Aquarium Ltd. 5 McGiven Drive, New Plymouth, RD1 New Zealand; in Japan by T.F.H. Publications, Japan—Jiro Tsuda, 10-12-3 Ohjidai, Sakura, Chiba 285, Japan; in SOUTH AFRICA by Lopis (Pty) Ltd., P.O. Box 39127, Booysens, 2016, Johannesburg, South Africa. Published by T.F.H. Publications, Inc.
MANUFACTURED IN THE UNITED STATES OF AMERICA
BY T.F.H. PUBLICATIONS, INC.

TAMING AND TRAINING LOVEBIRDS

RISA TEITLER
Professional Trainer

Above: *Front view of a masked lovebird.* **Opposite:** *Back view of a masked love-bird. Note the ideal type of strong, widely spaced wire necessary for a large love-bird flight.*

This book is intended as a guide for those who desire to own a tame pet lovebird. It is just as important to begin with a suitable candidate for taming as it is to follow through on the taming sessions. Read the sections on choosing and taming before picking out the prospective pet. If you follow the suggestions given, you should be able to show off your tame pet in a short time. Many thanks to Alvin T. Goldfarb and Stephen K. Curry for letting me photograph the beautiful lovebirds in their collection. Many of the more unusual hybrids are represented in their aviaries.

Below: *A pair of black-masked lovebirds. Many wild lovebirds build their nests in hollow tree trunks.* **Opposite:** *The peach-faced is the most common lovebird species found in captivity.*

Above: *A pair of Fischer's lovebirds.* **Opposite:** *A pair of black-masked lovebirds.*

Introduction

Lovebirds are small (approximately 5-6 inches long), colorful, playful birds that originate in Africa. They are very hardy and require a minimum of care and space. Many people enjoy them as ornamental birds; they provide a beautiful display on a screen porch or in a garden setting.

As tame pets they are very amusing, but the task of taming a lovebird is not easily accomplished unless you begin with a *very* young bird. Older birds live happily in a cage if given a balanced diet and enough room in the cage to exercise and fly around. Many people keep untamed birds loose in the house and feed them in a cage with the door always open. These birds fly around the house at will and return to the cage to eat and sleep. They can be a problem, however, if they decide to chew up the edges of your curtains or the door jambs. If you want a talkative, active, beautiful little bird that lives happily with virtually no attention, the lovebirds are for you.

For those who want an

Below: *A trio of Abyssinian lovebirds. The male bird has a patch of red on its head.* **Opposite:** *A red-faced lovebird.*

Above: *A pair of masked lovebirds.* **Opposite:** *A male Madagascar lovebird. The Madagascar is one of the rarer lovebird species.*

ornamental bird that they don't plan to tame, lovebirds are a good choice. In this case, however, it is recommended that you buy two birds. When buying two, it is good to get birds of the same species rather than one peach-faced and one black-masked, for example. Although you may mix the species, a larger, more aggressive lovebird like the peach-faced is likely to bully the smaller lovebird. Two lovebirds carry on an active relationship and are very interesting to observe. Often, two lovebirds that have access to a nestbox will spend a great deal of time playing in it, even if they aren't a true pair. It isn't unusual for two hens to build a nest and lay eggs. Of course these are infertile. Don't provide a nestbox if you want to exhibit the birds. Every time they see you approach they will run and hide in the box. If you want to try breeding lovebirds you will have to provide a nestbox and much more.

All of the lovebirds are native to Africa, its coastal islands and Madagascar. Some of the species and subspecies inhabit only a small area, but others range over a vast region. Lovebirds are all in the genus *Agapornis*. The most common lovebird in captivity is the peach-faced, *Agapornis roseicollis*. This is one of the larger lovebirds and one of the most aggressive. Peach-faced lovebirds should not be housed in the same cage with either a parakeet or a cockatiel. It has been the experience of the author that a peach-faced lovebird can harass even a blue and gold macaw!!

Fischer's lovebird, *Agapornis fischeri*, is also common in captivity. It is a beautiful lovebird, considerably smaller than the peach-faced, with a red bill and a large white periophthalmic (around the eye) ring. The face is orange and the body green.

Another common lovebird in captivity is the masked lovebird, *Agapornis personata*. The normal masked lovebird has a black face, yellow breast and green abdomen and wings. The bill is bright red. The periophthalmic ring is large and white. This variety has also been bred to blue, by eliminating the yellow factor. The blue-masked lovebird has a black face, but the body is a shade of turquoise blue.

The other lovebird species and subspecies are not common in captivity, but the hybrids of the common types abound. Lovebirds are avid breeders and, in the absence of mates of their own species, they cross freely. Many people maintain that the hybrid lovebirds are mules, incapable of reproducing. This is not the experience of the author. Hybrid babies mature and produce many beautiful offspring.

Lovebirds are extremely

The peach-faced is one of the most aggressive lovebird species, and it is also one of the largest.

sociable birds and will live and breed happily in a large community. There is not much documentation as to the life expectancy of lovebirds; they're parrots, so it is reasonable to expect them to live 15 to 25 years, if not longer, provided that adequate care is given.

It has not been the author's experience to meet with a talking lovebird. Although lovebirds chatter constantly they do not acquire speech as readily as some other members of the parrot group. Their comical behavior and

Above: *The Nyasa lovebird was once very popular, but it has been overshadowed by the easier-to-breed peach-faced lovebird. This bird is a lutino Nyasa lovebird.*
Opposite: *A normally colored Nyasa.*

expressive personalities, however, more than compensate for the lack of the spoken word.

Lovebirds are acrobatic geniuses. They will fly in bursts across the room, grab onto the edge of the curtains and do a somersault. If you provide a flying lovebird with a chain suspended from the ceiling, it will find the chain without coaxing and play on it for hours. Single birds will find their way to a mirror and then chatter and parade in front of their image. Anyone who has ever owned a lovebird and given it freedom in the house can tell you funny stories about the behavior of his pet.

Lovebirds are easy to maintain and can be found at most pet shops that sell birds. Prices vary according to the type of lovebird. For the common peach-faced you should expect to pay a fairly low price. The rare hybrids and normals of the rarer species cost considerably more than the peach-faced.

Because lovebirds are not easy to tame, the person who desires to have a tame pet lovebird will have to expect to spend a great deal of time and effort at the task. Whenever possible, try to buy a baby just out of the nest. A 5- to 6-week-old baby will not bite very hard, but the trainer must be a determined and cool thinker and have enough

A peach-faced lovebird and a hybrid of masked and peach-faced inside an outdoor aviary.

A peach-faced lovebird. This species is one of the easiest to find at pet shops, and it is one of the most reasonably priced varieties.

time to devote to the task.

The basic requirements for a single lovebird are an adequate cage, good quality feed, daily vitamin and mineral supplements, fresh water, fruits and vegetables. Routine cleaning of the cage and feeders is also required to keep the pet lovebird in good health.

Above: *A blue-masked lovebird.* **Opposite:** *A black-masked lovebird.*

Most pet lovebirds live with the family inside the home. They usually have a cage placed in the family room. It is not a good idea to place the cage near drafty windows or in the stream from air conditioners or electric heaters. You may have to adjust to the seasons by moving your bird's cage from one spot to another. Indirect sunlight is essential for good health, but direct sunlight can be harmful to the bird. Don't place the cage in the kitchen, where temperatures fluctuate. Avoid placing the cage next to the front or back door, for it will be in a draft every time the door opens.

Some people build attractive flight cages in their yards, complete with plants and running water. These displays can be beautiful if maintained properly. Always be careful when choosing plants for the aviary. Lovebirds are chewers and will chew most plants. Many household plants can harm a bird when ingested. Outdoor aviaries must be equipped with shelters for the birds to roost in. Shelters also protect the birds in bad weather. Ample shade from direct sunlight is necessary. Do not use a pond for the birds' water supply. Always provide fresh water for the birds on a daily basis.

When you plan to breed lovebirds in an outdoor community setting, you must place enough nestboxes into the flight to provide one for every pair, plus a couple of extras. This will help minimize fights over the boxes.

Use welded wire (1" x 1/2") or buy the commercially designed outdoor aviaries that are made for lovebirds and cockatiels. Ask your pet dealer to get these from his distributor. The welded wire aviary must be designed to keep out pests like rodents and neighborhood dogs and cats. Squirrels may look cute in the aviary until you discover that they are eating all of the food that you provide for the birds. Plan your homemade aviary before you begin to build. *Building an Aviary*, by C. Naether and Dr. M.M. Vriends, is an excellent text for the home builder.

Some lovebirds are kept in stores or elementary school classrooms. Although many individuals may adjust to these settings, others will always remain nervous. The steady bird is fine in the store or classroom, but the nervous birds that constantly fling themselves against the wire should be removed from these settings if they do not settle down in a reasonable amount of time. Give the bird two weeks to adjust

Opposite: *A peach-faced lovebird eating an unripe cherry. Be sure not to place any dangerous plants in your lovebird's cage or aviary.*

Above: *An Abyssinian lovebird.* **Opposite:** *A black-cheeked lovebird.*

to a new environment. If it remains frantic, take it home with you or give it to someone who will. It is unfair to subject the nervous bird to a lot of stress each day. Before bringing lovebirds into a class of very young children, remember that they can bite. The children must be supervised at all times when the bird is within reach.

You can keep lovebirds in a variety of settings as long as you provide good food and shelter from the elements. Don't think that you cannot keep a lovebird healthy in a cold climate. Of course, you cannot expect to winter the birds on your patio when snow is on the ground. Use your common sense. If you are warm enough, the birds are warm enough. If you need sweaters and jackets to keep warm, the lovebirds need some extra warmth also. Feed your birds well and keep them clean and warm and they should live happily for many years.

A peach-faced lovebird of the Dutch blue mutation. This variety has become quite common in recent years.

A pair of peach-faced lovebirds. If you don't have adequate time to spend with your lovebird, you may wish to consider purchasing a second bird. Be sure, however, that the birds will be compatible; keep an eye on them until they become accustomed to one another.

Above: *A red-faced lovebird. The red-faced lovebird nests in termite mounds.*
Opposite: *A black-collared lovebird. This species is sometimes called Swindern's lovebird.*

Left: *The blue mutation of the masked lovebird. If you plan to selectively breed your lovebirds, be sure to design a housing plan that allows you some control over the breeding pairs. Otherwise, you may end up with hybrids of unknown origin.* **Opposite:** *A pair of American pied light green peach-faced lovebirds.*

Lovebirds can live and thrive both indoors as caged pets and outdoors as aviary birds. When buying a suitable cage for the indoor pet, make sure that the wire is not too widely spaced or the bird will be going in and out at its convenience, not yours. The standard parakeet cage is not large enough for lovebirds. There are cages on the market made especially for lovebirds. Ask your pet dealer to show you lovebird cages in his equipment brochure, if you do not see them in the shop.

The cage should not measure less than 20″ square and 20″ high. Buy as large a cage as you can afford.

You may consider making your own cage. Buy 1″ x 1″ wire for larger lovebirds like the peach-faced. For the smaller lovebirds like the black-masked and Fischer's, buy 1″ x 1/2″. Again, the dimensions should not be smaller than 20″ square and 20″ high. Larger cages allow more flight space, which is desirable. The lovebirds are very active birds, and exercise space in the cage is

beneficial. All lovebird cages must be constructed of metal. Wooden cages will not last, for the birds will chew through them readily. Painted cages are not recommended.

You may hang your lovebird cage from a stand or a ceiling chain or just leave it on a small table. Wherever, put it in a spot that is easily viewed. Watching a lovebird play around is very amusing.

Perches should measure ¾" in diameter if you are using dowels. Natural wood perches are best, but make sure that they have not been sprayed with any chemicals. You can use branches from fruit trees, oak and elm—to name just a few possible sources of natural wood. Place two or three perches in the lovebird cage, but leave plenty of flight space. A

Pet stores everywhere carry a variety of cages designed especially for Lovebirds. There styles and colors available to fit every decor. Photo courtesy of Hagen.

small swing will often become a bird's roosting spot.

A cage cover is needed on cold nights but is not necessary on warm nights. You can make or buy your cage cover. Many lovebirds chew holes in their cage covers, so don't be surprised to find little spots chewed out of the cover.

The cups that come with parakeet cages are too small to hold the daily ration of feed for a normal lovebird. These hardy little birds eat a tremendous amount every day. You will need one cup for water, one cup for gravel and two cups for seed. One cup will hold sunflower and the other large seeds that you provide; the other will hold parakeet seed, oats, hemp and the smaller seeds. Cups can be made out of plastic, metal, glass and other easily cleaned materials. You can hang the feed cups from the sides of the cage or place them on the cage bottom. When using bottom feeders, make sure to place them in a spot that won't be soiled by the droppings.

The cage bottom can be covered with gravel paper, newspaper or sand. Sand is often messy, however.

Bird toys can be placed inside the cage as long as you do not

Bathing helps to keep a Lovebird's feathers in optimum condition. There are many different types of baths available at your local pet shop. Photo courtesy of Hagen.

clutter it. Commercially made playgrounds for lovebirds are available at well supplied pet shops.

Buying a Lovebird

Most people buy their lovebirds from a local pet shop. The most common pet shop lovebird is the peach-faced. If the shop is clean and offers a good selection of young birds (a young peach-faced lovebird has a gray face in addition to the black bill markings) at a reasonable cost, inquire further. Find out if the shop carries lovebird cages. *Don't* buy a standard parakeet cage. If you must go with parakeet wire buy a *very* large cage with room for larger feed and water dishes. A wire-top cage is better than a plastic top cage. Plastic bottoms don't last as long as metal ones.

Ask how they are feeding the birds. If the pet shop is feeding a balanced diet, their birds are most likely off to a good start in life. If the diet is deficient, the shop is not recommendable. The quality of feed and supplements that the shop offers will also indicate its suitability as a retail outlet for birds. Ask for the available literature on the type of bird that you are considering as a pet. Also inquire about who takes care of any sick or injured birds for the shop. Look at the amount of feed in the dishes. Is it fresh or a day or two days old? Does the water contain a vitamin supplement or is it clear? Is the cage bottom fairly clean or does it require new paper?

Another possible source from which to buy a lovebird is the hobbyist or breeder. The hobbyist will often sell you a handfed baby lovebird, and these are without question the best possible candidates for taming. Both hobbyists and breeders usually provide their birds with a rich diet and the best of supplements. They can give you good advice as to the care and handling of lovebirds. It is wise to inquire about who takes care of any sick or injured birds. You should get the name of a good vet when you purchase the bird.

Sometimes a friend or neighbor will offer to give you a lovebird. If the bird is healthy, go ahead and take it. Do not expect to have an easy time taming the bird if it is wild and an adult. It is better to keep such a bird well fed and in a large enough cage to allow some flying space. Under no circumstances should you put an older bird in with one that you have just purchased. If the newly purchased bird is a youngster, the older bird will most likely peck it severely. In front of your watchful eye, the older bird will do nothing. Once you leave them alone, however, the older bird will often

Opposite: *When purchasing a lovebird, be sure to check it carefully for signs of ill health. These peach-faced lovebirds seem to be in very good condition.*

A masked lovebird. Be sure to check the white eyerings (of lovebird species that have this trait) for problems. A healthy lovebird should have clear eyes and clean eyerings.

peck and sometimes kill the younger one. Avoid this by segregating the two birds. If you already have an untamed adult and you are given another untamed adult, it is possible to keep them together in the same cage. You must keep a close watch on them for the first couple of days to be certain that they do not fight. If they get along for the

first couple of days, chances are that they will become good friends. Be very cautious when introducing two lovebirds that have been living as single birds. The name lovebird is not altogether correct.

Transport the lovebird from pet shop to home in a small box with a couple of ventilation holes. Transporting the bird in a cage subjects it to undue stress. Every new sight and sound will frighten the bird and it will smash from one side of the cage to the other. By the time you get it home, you will have a frantic bird. The new cage should be set up and waiting *before* you bring the bird home. Place feed and water inside the cage and let the bird adjust to the surroundings. Once it eats its first full meal (usually not the first day), you can expect it to settle down quickly.

Don't transport the bird in rainy weather or on cold nights. Don't leave a bird in a closed car while you stop for lunch or shopping.

HOW TO CHOOSE THE BIRD

When you are lucky enough to buy a very young lovebird, don't worry too much about choosing between 5- or 6-week-old babies on the basis of personality. The great majority of *very* young birds will tame down quickly. The thing that you should look for

Vitamin and mineral supplements are an important part of a Lovebird's diet. Available in easy to administer forms, from powder and capsules to liquid, from pet shops everywhere. Photo courtesy of Hagen.

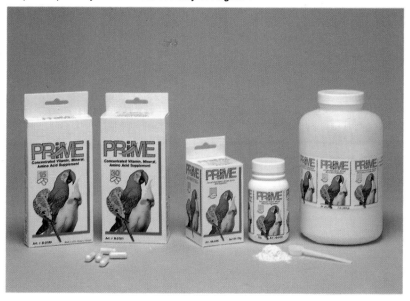

is a bird with *black markings on the bill.* Look for a baby with *smooth even plumage, clear, bright eyes* and an *alert* appearance. The *nostrils* should be open and free of dirt or discharge. The *chest* should be firm and full to the touch. (Be sure to feel the chest of a baby lovebird *before* you take it home.) The *feet* should have a firm, even grip when you place your finger between the toes. Lovebirds have four toes on each foot, and all toes should be present. The *vent* should be clean. *Droppings* on the cage bottom should be small, firm and dark in color, with a bit of white matter in them. Before grabbing the bird for examination, step back and observe its *respiration.* The breathing should be slow and even.

Sick lovebirds manifest many different symptoms and are usually easy to identify if you know what to look for.

A sick bird has dull or watery eyes. Its nose may be clogged or runny. You may hear it sneeze a few times. The bird will sit with feathers ruffled up and eyes closed if you observe it from a distance. Once you approach, it will jump into a pile with the others, making identification of illness symptoms difficult. The vent may be soiled with hard droppings or soft matter. Droppings on the cage bottom may be solid white, light green, yellow, brown, reddish or almost all water. The bird's breathing may be heavy or very shallow and rapid. When you feel its chest, the bird may be thin and have the breast bone protruding. Don't let anyone tell you that a baby bird is usually thin. This is not true. A healthy baby should have as full a chest as a healthy adult.

Lovebirds with cuts or wounds should not be purchased. Some species of lovebirds (such as the blue masked) have large white eye rings. The eye rings must not be puffy or have any discolorations or sores. Eye problems are often difficult to treat.

Opposite: *Fischer's lovebird is one of the species with the white periophthalmic ring.*

Spray Millet is enjoyed by all birds, especially Lovebirds. Given the opportunity these little parrots will gorge themselves, so keep plenty of it in hand! This nutritious treat is available from your local pet shop in various quantities. Photo courtesy of Hagen.

A good daily feeding plan includes both seed and fresh fruits and vegetables. You should feed both a good fresh sunflower seed and a good quality of parakeet seed. Either one by itself is not sufficient. In addition you should buy hemp, whole oats, spray millet and, if available, safflower seed. Mix a portion of these seeds into the parakeet and sunflower seed each day. Squirt a few drops of a good vitamin-mineral supplement onto the seed each day for the bird's plumage.

The fresh fruits can include apple, orange, banana, pineapple, peach, pear, melon and any other fruit in season. Vegetables that can be given are raw peas, green beans, squash, raw corn, carrots and others according to the bird's preference. These soft foods should be sprinkled with vitamin-mineral powder to provide a mineral supplement.

Each day you should provide a fresh green leafy vegetable such

as chicory or turnip tops. Head lettuce has no food value and is a waste of time. Celery tops are okay, but romaine lettuce is better. You can provide the same nourishment for the bird with the commercially available seedling grasses that your pet shop has, or you can take some parakeet seed and sprout it yourself. If the seed won't sprout, it has no value as hard seed either, so find another source for your feed.

You must also give the bird a good gravel mixture in a cup. If you want to sprinkle the gravel on the cage bottom, go ahead, but also provide a cup with gravel in it. Good gravel contains crushed granite (the white, sandy portion), crushed oyster shell, a small amount of charcoal (don't try to use charcoal briquettes or you will poison the bird) and some iodized table salt.

You must have a mineral block or a cuttlebone in the bird cage at all times. Replace these mineral supplements periodically. The water must be changed every day and the water cup cleaned thoroughly with hot water and soap. It is not enough to rinse the water cup with running water. You must scrub it out to remove any slick residues that form on the sides of the cup. This is one of the most important things that you can do to keep your bird healthy. Every day add a vitamin supplement to the drinking water. You can use any of the soluble vitamins that are manufactured for birds, but use them on a routine basis.

There is no need to give the bird beef or chicken—or any other table scrap for that matter. If you provide the bird with the type of balanced diet as outlined above, its requirements will be satisfied. If you *must* give the bird some of your dinner or dessert, make sure that it is neither too hot nor too cold, or you could create problems for the bird.

Treats for the lovebirds are fresh branches (including the leaves) washed and placed in the cage bars. Some lovebirds enjoy the seed bells that your pet shop markets for parakeets. The egg biscuits for parakeets can also be given. Spray millet, although part of the regular diet, can also be used as a treat or as a reward if you are attempting to teach a lovebird any tricks.

Opposite: *A lovely pair of Fischer's lovebirds. A healthy diet will go a long way toward keeping your lovebird beautiful and long-lived.*

General Care And Cleaning

Provide the bird with a shallow dish of warm water for its bath. This should be done in the morning and on sunny days only. On rainy days or when the sun is on its way down, the bath should be withheld. You may want to use a mister on the lovebird if it refuses to bathe. Give the bird every opportunity to discover the fun of taking a bath. You will enjoy watching it splash around and flap its wings in the water. When a lovebird is done bathing it will look really funny. The feathers will be all wet and of a brownish color, sticking out or down until the bird carefully preens each one back into its proper place.

There is no need to spray your lovebirds with a bug spray. House pets rarely have bugs, and if you keep the cage clean and sprayed you will accomplish the same end. Always use a spray that is manufactured especially for birds.

Feed lovebirds in the morning or afternoon, but whenever you feed, clean the cage bottom thoroughly. Look at the feed dishes; if they need cleaning, wash them in hot water and soap. Dry them before you put new seed in or you invite mold to form in the seed. Moldy seed can cause illness in the form of crop molds that could eventually kill the bird. By the same token, never feed lovebirds or any other bird fruit and vegetable matter that you wouldn't eat yourself. If it isn't good enough for you, it isn't healthy for a lovebird.

Clean the perches regularly with a perch scraper or a piece of sandpaper. You may want to use the sandpaper perch covers that your pet shop sells for parakeets, but these are not necessary. Keep feces and food residues off the cage wire by washing it with a sponge and clean water. Never use detergents on the cage wires unless you remove the bird, and then you should wash and rinse the whole cage. Remove all perches if you plan to do a major washing of the cage. Dry the cage completely before the bird goes back into it. If you wash the wooden perches (don't use plastic perches), be absolutely sure that they are very dry before replacing them in the cage. A bird that is forced to stand on wet or damp perches is subject to colds and arthritic conditions. Wash the cage bottom more often than the rest of the cage.

When you feel it necessary to clip the bird's claws, get all of the equipment together before you begin. You will need sharp clippers, a nail file, good light to work in and styptic powder in case

Opposite: *A peach-faced lovebird in a natural setting. The lovebird's environment must be kept clean and dry.*

you hit a vein. An experienced person can clip the claws without help, but a second person is always handy. Catch the bird in a net or towel and hold it with the head between your forefinger and middle finger. Rest the bird's body on your towel-covered lap. Use your other hand to hold its body still. The person clipping should clip one claw at a time and do all the claws on one foot before going to the other. Take just the tip off the claw. There is no need to take more than the tip unless the bird has badly overgrown claws. Even the overgrown claws should be clipped just a bit at a time or you risk hitting the vein. Clip all the claws and then file each nail with the nail file to smooth off the rough edges. If you hit the vein, take the styptic powder and press it against the bleeding claws. Hold it for a minute and then look to see if the bleeding has stopped. If it hasn't, repeat the application of powder. When bleeding has stopped, place

A pair of peach-faced lovebirds. When housing a number of birds together, be sure not to overcrowd them.

A black-cheeked lovebird. Perches and branches must be kept clean; they must also be replaced from time to time, as they wear down.

the lovebird back in his cage and leave him alone to rest. If you have natural wood perches in the cage instead of dowels, you may never have to clip the bird's claws.

Sometimes dirt gets into the bird's nostrils and has to be removed. Hold the bird securely, as if you were going to clip the claws. Take a toothpick and break off the point. Use a blunt edge to clean out the nares. You must be very careful not to harm the lovebird when cleaning out its nose. If the clog returns in a short time, you may have to suspect a cold. If so, see the vet or ask the pet shop for a commercially available antibiotic made for the treatment of colds in caged birds. If the cold gets worse or the medicine from the pet shops does not help, call the vet for advice.

Equipment For Taming

Unfortunately, no bird is immune to colds or respiratory problems. It is a good idea to have certain aids on hand in case of such emergencies. Medications for the most common ailments are available at your local pet shop. Photo courtesy of Hagen.

Opposite: *A pair of peach-faced lovebirds. A lovebird that is being tamed will be distracted if it has to share its cage with another bird.*

To tame a lovebird you will need a couple of *dowels,* about 12″ long, a bird *stand* and a prepared *taming area.* The taming area should be small enough to enable you to retrieve the bird without too much running around. Cover any mirrors or large windows in the taming area. Try to work in a room without a lot of furniture or you will be spending a lot of time chasing the lovebird out from under it. If the floor is not thickly carpeted, be certain to cover the floor with adequate *padding* to cushion any falls the bird might take during the taming less ons. Close the closets and the door of the room in which you are working. Give yourself at least one hour in the first taming session. Don't try to work the bird for 60 minutes continuously. Work for 10 or 15 minutes and then take a short rest. Continue in this manner until you are finished with the lesson. Later lessons may be

shorter, as long as you devote enough time to accomplish the task.

It is a waste of time to try to hand-train the bird inside its cage. Although you may accomplish it in the cage, you will probably receive more bites than you would in an open room.

You may feel it necessary to wear gloves when taming a lovebird. This is unlikely if you are at all experienced in bird-taming, but if you aren't, buy yourself a pair of very thin leather golf gloves in a neutral shade. The gloves should fit your hand securely or they won't protect you from the lovebird's bite. Never grab a bird even if you are wearing gloves. It is best to forget that you have them on. Stop wearing the gloves once the bird is hand tame.

Don't net the bird unless you must keep it from getting into trouble. Unless the bird is an escapee, the net should not be used to capture a bird and return it to his cage. A net has no place in the taming lesson.

If the lovebird gets hold of your finger and bites you, gently press against the corners of its mandibles. This should make the bird let go of you, but don't drop it to the floor. Kneel down to keep it from falling too far. Never press too hard against the mandibles. Remember that the lovebird is very small, even though its bite may seem very large. This is why it is so important to begin with a bird just out of the nest.

The Madagascar lovebird has no eyering and it has the smallest beak of all lovebirds.

A peach-faced lovebird. Always remember that the taming process requires patience and repetition, especially with an older bird.

Taming

When you want a tame pet, it is imperative that you buy a lovebird that shows black markings on the bill. This indicates that the lovebird is very young, just out of the nest. Once the black marks vanish from the upper bill the bird is at least two months old and is already difficult to tame. With other species of birds the age factor is not as critical, but with lovebirds you must get a very young bird if you plan to attempt taming.

First you must clip the bird's wing. Clip only one wing. Gather all of the necessary equipment and study the accompanying descriptions of wing clipping before you begin. You will need a pair of small wire cutters, a pair of scissors and a towel, net or glove. Two people must work together to clip the bird's wing. First catch the bird with a net, towel or glove. Then hold it so that its head is between your forefinger and middle finger. Your ring finger and pinkie should wrap around the bird's back to support it. Your thumb should provide the bird a perch for its feet. Lovebirds are wiggly little birds, so be certain to hold the bird securely to avoid getting bitten. Since lovebirds are so small and light, an extensive clipping job is needed to keep them from flying. Even clipped, your lovebird will amaze you at how well it can maneuver from one place to another.

To clip the bird's wing, pull out both wings one at a time and examine the feathers. If there are blood feathers present on one wing, leave it as it is and look at the other wing. Blood feathers are new feathers that still have a blood vein inside the quill for nourishment. These feathers must never be clipped off. If you clip a blood feather the bird will begin to bleed from the quill and you must take action to stop the flow of blood. Use styptic powder in such an emergency. Clip the wing that has no blood feathers present.

Hold the wing securely at the bend. Don't overextend it, but hold it out firmly so that you can see the underside of the wing feathers clearly. Push away the undercovert feathers to expose the quills of the flight feathers. Leave the first two feathers on the end of the wing as they are. Clip off the rest of the flight feathers, leaving one or two feathers next to the bird's torso. Clip each feather at the point at which the feather begins to grow out of the shaft. Leave at least three-quarters inch of the quill sticking out of the wing. *Never cut the feathers off at the point where they emerge from the*

Opposite: *A peach-faced lovebird in flight. To prevent a nervous lovebird from flying away from you during the taming session, it may be necessary to clip the wings.*

wing. By so doing you leave the edge of the wing unprotected, and if the lovebird hits the edge of the wing it could damage feather follicles. Be careful to clip the feathers far enough away from the edge of the wing to provide a cushion for the wing against impacts.

When you are finished with the job of clipping the wing, bring the lovebird into the prepared taming area and place it on the floor. You are now ready to begin the task of taming.

Take a wooden dowel and press against the bird's chest. It will probably try to fly away from you. Don't chase after it. Wait until it comes to a rest and then approach it again with the dowel. A young bird will usually step onto the dowel in a few minutes. Slowly move the dowel toward you and talk to the bird to reassure it. Place your hand in front of it and gently push against its legs. The bird will either step on or try to fly away. If it flies, begin again with the dowel. Repeat this procedure

A pair of American white peach-faced lovebirds perched on a wooden dowel. The dowel is an essential piece of equipment for the taming process.

A lutino peach-faced lovebird. After a few taming sessions, the bird will become accustomed to the dowel; it will then be ready for the process of hand-taming.

until the lovebird steps onto your hand. Let it sit there for a minute and then make it step back onto the dowel. Drill the bird in this manner—dowel to hand, hand to dowel—until the bird steps onto both without hesitation. Once this is accomplished, begin to drill the bird stepping from one hand to the other. You can now place the bird on a low stand and practice having it step onto your hand and back to the stand. It is not absolutely necessary for you to perch-train a lovebird, but it

certainly makes it much easier in the long run to place your bird in the family room on a stand and not worry about having to handle it every minute while it is out of the cage.

When you are attempting to tame a baby lovebird, one with black markings on the bill, you should be able to accomplish the task in an amazingly short amount of time. Young birds are very versatile and adjust to new situations readily. In just a couple of days your baby lovebird will be easy to handle. An older bird would take considerably more time and patience.

If the newly tamed young bird does not step onto your hand when it is in the cage, try getting it out on a stick. Once it is out of the cage, you can place it on your hand and continue your taming lessons.

Offer the lovebird some spray millet. See whether it will take a sunflower seed from your hand. Try touching it on the chest or the back of the neck.

When you are attempting to tame an older lovebird, be prepared to spend much more time at the task than you would with a baby. Some lovebirds will bite so hard and so consistently that you will decide to let them live their lives however they want to. This is nothing to feel bad about. The bite of the tenacious little lovebird is very painful, and some older birds just refuse to be tamed. To begin the task with an older bird you should wear some protection on your hands. Use flesh-tone or white gloves that fit your hand securely. Loose gloves don't give you as much protection.

Work in a small area. Do a great deal of stick work with the older lovebird. When you have really drilled the bird with the stick to the extent that it jumps onto the stick when it is pushed against the bird's chest, you can begin to use your hand. Push against the chest

firmly with an upward motion. If the bird bites, press your thumb and forefinger against the juncture of the mandibles. Don't press too hard. A firm press should make the bird release. If this doesn't work, try rolling your finger away from the bird and press against the mandibles at the same time. Your last resort is to pry the bird's bill off your finger and begin again. Keep cool and don't injure the bird.

With a consistent biter, try a strict food reward situation. During taming sessions give the bird sunflower seed from your hand as it steps onto the stick. Soon you can give the same reward for stepping onto your hand. Try using spray millet as a reward. Most lovebirds love millet spray. You may also have to employ a feeding schedule for the stubborn lovebird. Leave water in the bird's cage at all times, but remove the food. Measure its daily ration into a separate cup and use it during your taming lesson. If the bird refuses to eat the seed and just takes it and drops it on the floor, don't worry. It may take a couple of days before the bird is willing to take the seed from your hand. If this is the case, give it only half the normal ration for dinner. After one hour remove the feed dish, clean it out and replace it in the cage empty. Don't let your bird go without food completely, but you may find it helpful to restrict its

Artist's rendering of a blue mutation of the masked lovebird.

intake if it refuses to eat from your hand and insists on biting you. *Do not* restrict the feed with a new lovebird immediately. First try taming it as though it were a youngster. In addition, it is foolish to take the food from a bird until it has adjusted to eating a normal ration in new surroundings. In fact it will be impossible for you to determine what the bird's normal ration is until you have observed its eating habits for at least a week. Once you know how much the bird eats when restricted, you can decide what constitutes its normal daily intake. Don't try to guess at the amount or you may cause yourself more trouble than it is worth.

With an older lovebird you may be able to accomplish only stick and perch training. Some older birds may become fairly tame and even pettable, but your best bet for a tame, kissable lovebird is to start with a very young bird.

Always do the initial taming by yourself in a prepared area. The presence of other people will distract both you and the bird. Never lift the bird high off the floor in the initial taming; wait until the lovebird sits quietly and securely on your hand. Remember to remain calm when the bird tries to fly away from you. Don't rush after it. Wait until it lands before you attempt to get it back under control. Repetition is the key to successfully taming a young lovebird.

Once the bird is tame to one member of the household, other family members can have the bird sit on their hands. The bird will soon find its way to the family room and sit quietly on its perch if you train it correctly. Hang a toy from the bird stand to keep the lovebird occupied. Lovebirds are very curious, active birds. You must provide them with suitable activity or they will provide their own, possibly not to your liking.

Never leave the bird unattended for long periods of time. It could get into all sorts of mischief before you return. Keep the lovebird away from open windows and doors. Even a clipped bird can make a handy escape.

A masked lovebird. Taming sessions are a wonderful way for the lovebird and its owner to become acquainted with each other.

How Tame Can A Lovebird Become?

Left: *An American yellow peach-faced lovebird.* **Opposite:** *A Dutch blue peach-faced lovebird.*

When you begin with a little baby just out of the nest, or when you have the opportunity to obtain a hand-fed baby lovebird, you can expect to have a *very* tame bird. With proper and consistent handling a lovebird will become quite affectionate toward its owner. It will allow itself to be petted, turned on its back, grabbed and roughed up a bit— and will even enjoy a kiss or two!

The tame baby will play in your hair and climb into your pocket for a bit of food. It will play tug-of-war with you and ride around on your shoulder wherever you go. If there is a dog in the household, you may find that the lovebird will like to sit on his back and play with his collar, provided that he is a steady dog. No other family pets are safe from the attentions of a lovebird. They are such curious little birds that they investigate each and every thing in the house, living and inanimate.

The tame lovebird can be taught a few simple tricks. It is best to capitalize on the bird's

How Tame Can A Lovebird Become?

natural antics when deciding on a repertoire of tricks. Teach it to climb a ladder and receive a reward in a cup at the top. Teach it to climb down a rope into a cup for a sunflower seed. It can learn to place items into a cup or remove them. Hang a bell from a crossbar and teach the bird to ring it for a reward. All of these tricks are really designed around the natural behavior of lovebirds. It is up to the trainer to observe the individual bird and structure a learning situation for it.

It is unlikely that you will be able to get your lovebird to verbalize, but you may want to toy with trying to get it to chirp for a seed. With very persistent training

A tame masked lovebird. A tame bird will allow itself to be held in such a fashion. This makes it easier for the owner to check the bird's nails, clip its wings, etc.

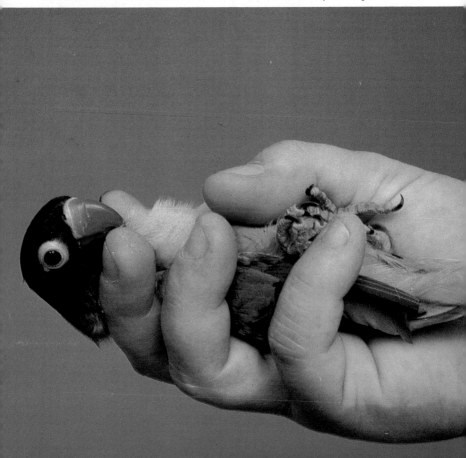

Artist's rendering of grey-headed lovebirds.

a lovebird may acquire one or two words and a wolf whistle. This process usually takes much more time and effort than most people are willing to exert. Lovebirds should not be considered "good" talkers.

The red splotches on the body of this peach-faced lovebird may be caused by dietary deficiencies.

These two photos show a green pied peach-faced lovebird.

When you buy your lovebird you should also invest in some first aid preparations in case of accident or illness. If you have an untamed bird and you have to examine it for a wound, use a towel or glove to hold it. If your bird is tame, these precautions should not be necessary. Get some hydrogen peroxide from the drug store and keep it on hand in case the bird is wounded or breaks a feather or a claw. Also obtain a styptic powder from your pet shop; the powder is used to stop bleeding if you cannot control it with peroxide. It is a *powdered* medication; do not confuse it with a styptic pencil, which is too hard to work effectively on birds. Get some antiseptic powder to dress wounds once they have been cleaned with peroxide.

You may have sterile cotton balls in the house. These should be used to clean wounds. Buy a commercially marketed bird salve to use as a dressing and on dry feet. Always gather the needed medical preparations before you catch the bird to examine it.

For *wounds*, pick up the bird and examine it. You may need another person to assist you. Wash the wound with hydrogen peroxide. If the wound continues to bleed, use a cotton ball with peroxide to press against the bleeding spot. Hold it against the wound for at least a couple of minutes to permit clotting. If

necessary use the styptic powder to stop severe bleeding. Again, use a cotton ball for pressure when needed. Dress the open wound with antiseptic powder. You may have to consult a vet for follow-up care. Don't drag a bleeding bird to the veterinarian without trying to stop the bleeding yourself.

For *twisted legs, toes and feet,* place the perches low in the cage and food and water close enough to permit the bird access without climbing around. If the leg or foot is not being used by the lovebird in 24 hours, you can call the vet for an appointment or try to treat the bird yourself. Hold the bird, with the affected leg or foot under a stream of warm (not hot) running water from the tap. This is a way of stimulating the circulation. Give the running water treatment for 3 to 5 minutes. Be careful not to get the bird wet all over. Dry the leg and foot well before replacing the bird in the cage. Do not try bandaging the leg. This will annoy the bird and cause it to tear off the bandage. If the lovebird is not using the leg in three days, you should definitely see the vet.

Broken blood feathers and

Opposite: *A peach-faced lovebird. The lovebird's environment should be designed with the bird's health and safety in mind.*

Above and opposite: *A blue variety of the peach-faced lovebird, shown from two different angles.*

bleeding claws must be treated with styptic powder. Take a small amount of the powder and press it into the bleeding spot with your finger. Hold it there for a minute. Pull your finger away and watch. If bleeding does not break through the powder, place the bird back in its cage and keep it quiet. In the case of broken blood feathers, it may be necessary to extract the broken feather, but initially the most important thing is to stop the bleeding. Sometimes the feather will bleed every time the bird flaps its wing. This is the right time to see the vet. Have the feather pulled by a vet or professional bird handler.

Eye problems are not uncommon with lovebirds. Disorders of the eye must be treated by a vet. Do not attempt to treat these problems by yourself.

A pair of Fischer's lovebirds. Healthy birds should never be kept near a contaminated bird, as contagion can spread very quickly throughout an aviary.

A Dutch blue ino peach-faced lovebird. This color variety was once referred to as "cream."

Eyes can become swollen from infections or injuries. Sometimes sore areas may appear on the large white ophthalmic ring. These sores may be a disease in themselves or the symptoms of some other disorder.

Broken legs and *wings* occur as the result of injury. The bird can get into mischief while playing by itself, or the injury can occur while you are handling it. Whenever a lovebird is suspected of sustaining a broken limb, be sure to get it into a warm cage with the perches

lowered and food and water within reach. The bird must be kept in a restricted space to immobilize the broken limb. It is a good idea to restrict the bird's view by covering the cage. Although broken bones are clearly revealed by X-rays, there is no practical reason for taking the bird to the veterinarian unless the bone has broken through the outer layer of skin. Since most vets would not try to splint a fracture on a lovebird, the trip could do the bird more harm than good. However, if the break

Above: *A pair of kissing peach-faced lovebirds. The lovable attitude of these birds, and their constant attention to each other, became the basis for their name.* **Opposite:** *A yellow variety peach-faced lovebird with its owner, Cliff Witt.*

is complicated by other factors (the bone protruding through the skin for example), be sure to see the vet.

Some birds develop *feather disorders* as a result of poor diet. Others may begin to chew their feathers for no apparent reason. If your bird molts continually, you should suspect either overheating or an imbalance in the diet. Review the chapter on diet and, if you are not feeding correctly, adjust. Be sure to supply the lovebird with vitamin and mineral supplements as well as fresh branches to chew. Feather problems are rare with the lovebirds, so if you have such a problem, diet is probably the answer.

Lovebirds can contract the *common cold* just as humans do. Their eyes water, their noses run and they get sore throats. If the bird is healthy and eating well, the right medication should help it throw off the cold with no after-effects. Left untreated, the common cold can develop into pneumonia, asthma, aspergillosis and other chronic respiratory conditions. Most vets will prescribe antibiotic drugs to combat the common cold. Often your pet shop will carry antibiotic preparations for use with caged birds. Don't treat your lovebird for

An Abyssinian lovebird hen. Only healthy lovebird hens should be considered for breeding purposes.

An American pied Dutch blue peach-faced lovebird. This variety is sometimes referred to as the "buttermilk" in Great Britain.

every sneeze, but if it sneezes continually and loses its appetite, looks droopy and other symptoms appear, it is good to consult with the vet. He may suggest that you use the pet shop drug or ask you to bring the bird in for examination. Always keep the lovebird extremely warm when it has a cold; 90 to 95°F. is not too hot. Follow the directions on the pet shop drug or follow the directions of your vet accurately. See to it that your bird eats. Give it as much as it likes of whatever

it likes.

A lovebird with *diarrhea* is an unhappy bird. Usually the soft food in the diet is blamed for causing diarrhea. This is a false assumption. If the diet is well balanced it *should* contain soft food. When soft food is suddenly introduced into the diet, diarrhea may result, but usually this is a symptom of a digestive disorder. Anti-diarrhea preparations may be available at your pet shop. If not, call your vet for a prescription. Some people treat their birds with

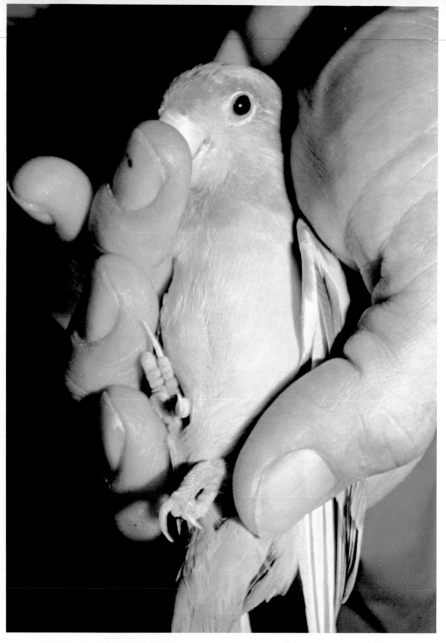

Above: *A pied peach-faced lovebird has dark blue, light blue, green and yellow feathers.* **Opposite:** *A lutino mutant peach-faced lovebird is missing the blue pigment and thus has only yellow, red, and white feathers.*

molasses in the water. This home remedy often works for birds.

When the bird is unable to void, *constipation* should be suspected. Treat the bird with Sal Hepatica, a teaspoon to a quart of boiled water. Allow the water to cool and serve it for three days. Mix it fresh every day. If this does not help, see the vet.

Parasites are rarely a problem with caged household pets, but if your bird eats a great deal and still loses weight, you should suspect internal parasites. Take a sample of the bird's droppings to the vet for examination. Call him first to find out how fresh the sample must be. Usually the vet will ask for a sample no more than eight hours old.

Wheezing is the symptom of respiratory trouble. If your lovebird is *wheezing*, see the vet immediately. Do not waste time trying over-the-counter preparations from the pet dealer. Once the bird is wheezing, action must be taken or the bird may die. Keep it extremely warm, about 95 degrees. Keep food in front of it at all times and transport the bird in a closed box to the vet.

Tumors, lumps and bumps should be examined by the vet for accurate diagnosis and proper treatment.

Overgrown claws and *beaks* should be trimmed to help the bird grip the perch easily and correctly and to enable it to eat its fill. See

an experienced bird handler or the vet to have the claw and bill trimmed if overgrown.

Scales around the eyes and bill are usually due to the presence of the scaly mite, an external parasite. See your pet dealer for a remedy. Read the directions carefully. The preparations for scaly mite are very strong, and you must be careful not to get them into the bird's eyes or mouth. Keeping the bird and its cage clean is the best prevention for scaly mite.

Shock is usually the result of injury. Keep the bird warm and quiet. There is no reason to take it to the vet for diagnosis. If the shock is not too severe, the bird should come out of shock in a few minutes to a few hours. Often shock can be the immediate cause of death, so keep the bird warm and don't handle it too much if you suspect shock. Breathing becomes shallow, and the bird's eyes do not focus. Sometimes a bird makes a moaning or chirping sound. Recognize the symptoms and learn to treat the condition.

Suspect internal *parasites* if your bird begins to eat an enormous amount of feed and appears to lose weight. Although most house pets that are kept clean should never develop parasite infestation, the lovebirds kept outdoors may. Bring a fresh stool sample to the vet for examination. The sample must be

In the yellow varieties of the peach-faced lovebird, the plumage looks yellowish green rather than yellow. The rump is pale bluish to white in color.

fresh to ensure accurate diagnosis. The vet can prescribe medicines that will effectively eradicate parasites.

Whenever a bird stops eating or stops eliminating waste or is found to be very thin, with the breast bone protruding, see the vet immediately.

Opposite: *A green pied peach-faced lovebird.* **Above:** *A very rare lovebird color variety, the silver.*

Breeding Lovebirds

Lovebirds are among the easiest birds to breed in captivity. They are good subjects for the beginner. Always try to make sure that the birds are unrelated. Although related birds may raise young, their babies will be subject to the genetic flaws that can result from inbreeding. Controlled inbreeding is responsible for the development of the more interesting hybrid lovebirds that are appearing regularly. The aviculturists who practice controlled inbreeding must do their homework in genetics to ensure that they do not develop undesirable traits in the offspring of such unions.

Trying to determine that you do indeed have a true pair of lovebirds, a male and female, is not always easy. There are no physical differences in appearance between the male and female. Some people find it necessary to obtain four or five birds before they are sure of getting a good pair. These birds are placed together in a community cage and observed. When two birds consistently stay together and preen one another's feathers, keep their distance from the other birds and eat and sleep together, it can be safely assumed that they are a pair. You may observe the birds mating. Such pairs can be provided with a nestbox and bred in the community cage provided that it is

large enough. There must be room enough for the birds that are not breeding to steer clear of the breeding pair. Make the community cage 4 feet high, 3 feet long and 2 feet wide for six birds. The greater the number of pairs in the cage the larger the cage must be. Use 1-inch by 1-inch wire mesh for the peach-faced lovebirds. The smaller lovebirds like the black-masked and Fischer's require 1-inch by ½-inch wire mesh. Larger wire invites escape and accident. The smaller birds may try to squeeze through the larger mesh and get caught. Eyes can be damaged and wings can be broken. Use the right wire mesh for the species you have.

Commercially marketed community lovebird cages may be displayed by your pet dealer. If not, ask whether these cages are obtainable on special order.

Nestboxes are the same size and construction as are used for parakeets and are available at all well stocked pet shops. Usually they are made of wood and are mounted on the outside of the breeding cage. Boxes made of pressed cardboard should not be used for lovebirds. The birds may chew out pieces of the bottom or sides.

Provide the birds with nesting materials. People who live in Florida and California have a ready supply of nesting material in the form of palm fronds. Palm

Artist's rendering of a trio of parrots: red-rumped parrot, lutino Nyasa lovebird, and blue-masked lovebird.

Right: *A blue pied mutation of the peach-faced lovebird.*
Opposite: *A pair of peach-faced lovebirds with their youngsters in a colony breeding setup.*

fronds are used readily by lovebirds. The fronds are run back and forth through the bill, softened and chewed into short pieces that are stuck into the wing, tail and body feathers of the birds. When loaded up with a good supply the birds fly to their nests and weave the material together into a cup shape. There they lay their eggs and raise their young. When palm fronds are not available, provide the birds with small cuttings from non-poisonous plants and trees. Make sure that the cuttings have not been sprayed with insecticide. The lovebirds will strip the bark, chew the twigs into pieces and carry them to the box. There they will construct a rough cup-shaped nesting area.

Lovebirds are reproductively mature before one year of age. Birds under six months old should not be set up in a breeding situation. The birds must be in good health and plumage. They should not be going through a molt when you set up their nestbox. Make sure that the diet is well balanced and that the birds are eating well before you set up the nestbox. Provide plenty of leafy green vegetables when the birds begin to settle down to nest. Your birds may begin to devour apple, orange and corn even though they hardly touched it before. Give the regimen of vitamin and mineral supplements as outlined in the section on

feeding. Do not wait until the babies hatch to provide the additional soft foods and supplements.

Lovebirds will breed all year round in almost any weather when housed indoors. The outdoor aviary birds will adjust their breeding to climatic variations.

To begin the breeding season, make cleaned and sprayed nestboxes accessible to the lovebirds. Begin beefing up the diet. If you have a true pair in breeding condition, they could go to nest in a remarkably short period of time. At present, the author has a pair of black-masked lovebirds on a nest of six eggs just one month after acquiring them.

To end the breeding season, remove the nestboxes from the cage and seal up any holes you have made in the cage. Over-breeding the birds by giving them no off-season results in progressively weaker offspring.

The normal clutch can be from three to eight eggs. When there are seven or eight eggs in the nest it is unlikely that all will be hatched and reared by the parents. Incubation is carried out almost entirely by the hen and varies considerably from pair to pair. Some lovebirds may hatch out their chicks in 16 days while others may take 23 to 24 days. Once the babies arrive the parents begin feeding them vigorously. Feeding sounds can be heard

An olive peach-faced lovebird. This variety is of a much darker green color than is the normal variety.

distinctly. The parents stuff their chicks until they look as if they may burst. The dependency period lasts 4½ weeks, and the chicks begin weaning immediately after first emerging from the box. For the first two or three nights the babies return to the nest at night. After that they spend their nights huddled together in the outer cage. Parents continue to feed these babies for less than one week, at which time it is safe to remove the babies from the nest and place them into a nursery cage.

Observe the youngsters to make sure that they are all getting enough to eat on their own. You should provide soft food for the babies as well as hard seed. At first they will just pick at the seed and eat all the soft food. Soon they will begin to demolish the servings of sunflower and parakeet seed that you have provided. At this point the lovebirds are completely weaned and ready to go to new homes as pets.

Opposite: *Cliff Witt with one of his precious, well-trained lovebirds. This bird was hand fed.* **Top:** *A nest of three masked lovebirds.* **Bottom Right:** *A lovebird loves to bathe.* **Bottom Left:** *Note how wet this lovebird's feathers look after a bath.*

When you find that a baby is not being fed by the parents it is probable that you will have to hand-rear the bird or let it die. Sometimes the parents detect a flaw in the chick and refuse to feed it, meanwhile feeding the rest of the chicks with relish. If this is the case it is unlikely that your efforts at hand-rearing will succeed. Another reason for inadequate feeding is inexperience. The lovebirds that have just hatched their first chicks may not be sure of what to do with them and let the babies die. The next clutch is often cared for unerringly.

To hand-feed a young lovebird, try using baby pablum and prepared baby vegetables. Use warm water to bring the ingredients to the proper consistency. *Never* feed cold food to the chicks or you may kill them. Remember that warm baby food cools rapidly, so float your dish in a cup of very hot water. The heat will penetrate through the dish and keep the soft baby food warm. Also be careful not to feed food that is too hot or you may burn the chick. Feedings must be given regularly every two to three hours when the chicks are less than one week old. Use your common sense to determine how soon you can stretch the feedings out to four to five hours. As the babies grow they will require more food but less frequent feedings. At 4½ weeks you should begin to wean the babies. Provide them with a dish of soft foods, one of parakeet seed and one of water with soluble vitamins. Let the babies sit in the nursery cage with the feed until afternoon and then give them a good feeding by hand. If you feed them by hand first thing in the morning it will take longer to wean them. Once weaned, the chicks may refuse to take any part in your efforts at handfeeding.

The chicks begin to fly at about four weeks of age. You may hear them flapping their wings inside the nestbox before they come out or, if hand-rearing, you will see them begin to flap their wings rapidly while remaining in the same place. Soon, however, they will be up and away. For safety, place the hand-reared young in a cage before they begin flying around.

Index

Taming and Training Lovebirds
KW-038